Duties and Responsibilities

OF DIRECTORS OF NOT-FOR-PROFIT ORGANIZATIONS

Hugh M. Kelly, Q.C.

THIRD EDITION

Published by
Canadian Society of Association Executives
10 King Street East, Suite 1100
Toronto, Ontario M5C 1C3
www.csae.com

Copyright © 2012 Canadian Society of Association Executives

All rights reserved. No part of the publication may be reproduced or transmitted in any form or by any means, electronic or mechanical, including photocopy, recording or any information storage and retrieval system, without permission in writing from the publisher.

This publication is published for informational and educational purposes only and should not be considered legal advice. Any use of the information contained in this publication is the sole responsibility of the reader.

Library and Archives Canada Cataloguing in Publication

Kelly, Hugh M.

    Duties & responsibilities of directors of not-for-profit organizations / by Hugh M. Kelly. -- 3rd ed.

Includes bibliographical references.

ISBN 978-0-9811910-9-6

    1. Directors of corporations--Legal status, laws, etc.--Canada. 2. Nonprofit organizations--Canada. 3. Risk management--Canada. I. Canadian Society of Association Executives II. Title. III. Title: Duties and responsibilities of directors of not-for-profit organizations.

KE1373.K44 2012	346.71'064	C2011-908649-2
KF1388.7.K45 2012		

    3   4   5   6   7   8   9 10

Printed in Canada

csae | scda®
CANADIAN SOCIETY OF ASSOCIATION EXECUTIVES
SOCIÉTÉ CANADIENNE DES DIRECTEURS D'ASSOCIATION

Contents

PREFACE	5
IMPORTANT NOTE	7
INTRODUCTION	9
Purpose	9
Legislative Overhaul	9
Unique Characteristics of Not-For-Profit Corporations	10
Distinction Between the Corporation and its Persons	10
Meetings	11
Minutes	11
Culture	12
Profit	12
Directors' Liability Exposure	13
Risk Management	13
ROLE OF DIRECTORS	15
DUTIES OF DIRECTORS	17
Duty of Knowledge	17
Duty of Care	18
Duty of Skill and Prudence	19
Duty of Diligence	20
Duty to Manage	21
Fiduciary Duty	21
Duties as Trustees	22
Investment Powers	22
Delegation by Directors	23
Duty to Avoid Conflicts of Interest	24
Duty to Act Within Scope of Authority	25

LIABILITIES OF DIRECTORS	**27**
Criminal Liability	27
Civil Liability	27
Statutory Liabilities	28
Employee and Workplace Liability	29
Income Tax Liability	29
Environmental Liability	31
Business Practices	32
PROTECTION OF DIRECTORS	**33**
Indemnification	33
Insurance	35
Independent Advice	36
Disclosure of Competing Interests	36
Impact of Ratification	36
Due Diligence	37
AN EFFECTIVE BOARD OF DIRECTORS	**39**
Checklist	39
Checklist Caution	40
ENDNOTES	**41**
ABOUT THE AUTHOR	**45**

Preface

In 1988, the Canadian Society of Association Executives (CSAE) published a resource for directors of not-for-profit organizations to help them understand their legal duties and responsibilities. During the next 10 years, there was a dramatic growth in interests in corporate governance both in the private and not-for-profit sectors.

In 1999, CSAE published a monograph entitled *Duties and Responsibilities of Directors of Not-for-Profit Corporations*, aimed at directors of not-for-profit organizations in Canada. Co-authored by Hugh M. Kelly, Q.C., and Mark R Frederick, this publication quickly became a bestseller for CSAE, with more than 10,000 copies sold. Its second edition, published in 2004, has continued to be widely recognized as the primer for board directors and an invaluable resource for organizations in board orientation sessions.

Hugh Kelly has returned to provide this third edition of the publication for 2012, which includes important updates and information resulting from recent legislative changes. Like the 2004 version, and the one before it, this new edition is designed to provide directors of not-for-profit organizations with information about potential liability they may face in their role as director. Informing them of their responsibilities should be a key element of any annual orientation program.

Important Note

This publication is not, and is not intended to be, legal advice, and should not be considered or treated as such. Readers are cautioned that this publication can only address general, not particular, situations, which may assist in determining when a person moves into a sphere in which legal issues must be addressed. Legal advice is dependent upon the particular facts in a specific situation, and the application of the appropriate laws and legal principles to that situation. A director or officer may find general information in this publication but, depending on the importance of the issue involved, may need to seek appropriate independent legal advice.

Note also that with the increasing complexity of legislation and corporate activity in which not-for-profit organizations engage, it is not possible in a publication such as this to explore every requirement and nuance that a director or officer might face. Therefore, the more frequent and common issues are addressed, and the text necessarily excludes many important issues that may face a lesser number of organizations.

Introduction

Purpose

The purpose of this publication is to highlight some of the important duties and liabilities of directors of not-for-profit corporations, as well as ways in which directors may successfully avoid personal liability. In recent years, the term "risk management" has become top of mind for those considering issues of corporate governance, spurred on in part by the scandals that emerged in the United States from highly inappropriate activity by corporate directors and/or officers in a number of large organizations.[1] This publication is a sort of road map for how directors may go about managing the risk that they have as directors, enabling them to avoid such unpleasant situations.

Further resources are available from CSAE with respect to board effectiveness—a topic that is beyond the scope of this publication.

Legislative Overhaul

Since the previous edition of this publication, the Parliament of Canada and the Legislature of Ontario have completed the overhaul of the legislation governing not-for-profit corporations. At the date of publication, although both have been given Third Reading and Royal Assent, only the *Canada Not-for-profit Corporations Act*[2] ("Canada NFP Act") is in force; the Ontario *Not-for-Profit Corporations Act, 2010*[3] ("Ontario NFP Act") is not yet in force. While an exploration of the full impact of these statutes is beyond the scope of this publication, organizations incorporated under the *Canada Corporations Act*[4] and the *Ontario Corporations Act*[5] as non-share capital corporations will be subject to, and need to take action as prescribed in, these new statutes upon their respective proclamations.

Introduction

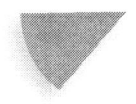

Unique Characteristics of Not-for-Profit Corporations

Not-for-profit corporations[6] have many characteristics in common with business corporations, and many of the reasons[7] for incorporating not-for-profit corporations are shared by their business counterparts.[8] Readers who are accustomed to commercial corporations will find much familiar content in this publication. A few features of not-for-profit corporations are unique.

Like its commercial corporation counterpart, a not-for-profit corporation is a separate legal person, composed of:

- members (the equivalent of shareholders in a commercial corporation);
- directors elected by the members (as in a commercial corporation); and
- officers appointed by the directors (as in a commercial corporation).

There is a true distinction between the corporation itself (the separate legal person), the persons who are directors, the persons who are officers, and the persons who are members.

Distinction Between the Corporation and its Persons

In many not-for-profit corporations, persons become members by application to and approval by the existing board of directors, and generally in Canada, the members elect directors. In some jurisdictions, it is permitted that a number of the directors may become directors by virtue of holding another office—that is, *ex officio* directors[9] — or become directors by appointment by the remaining directors (subject to restrictions).[10]

Once elected to the board of directors, it is the board as a collective—rather than individual directors—that has the power and obligation to manage the affairs of the corporation.

Meetings

In the narrow sense, the corporation itself does not hold any meetings. The members hold meetings and the board of directors holds meetings. In both cases, the two groups act by means of resolutions enacted or passed in accordance with the bylaws of the corporation governing its operations.

As one of its obligations, the board of directors must call the annual meeting of members of the corporation, fixing the date, time, and place within the limits authorized in the corporation bylaws. As already noted, the annual meeting is a meeting of the corporation members, not a meeting of the corporation. The business of this meeting is prescribed in part by law and in part by the corporation bylaws. Included generally (whether or not mandated) in the business of the annual meeting are the consideration of the financial statements, the receipt of the report of the auditor,[11] the receipt of the report of the administration, the appointment of the auditor, and the election of the directors. Other business may emerge but these matters are required.

Once the directors are elected, it is customary for the board of directors to convene for the purpose of organizing, including the election of officers and the composition of standing and other committees. Additional business varies according to the exigencies of the moment and/or in accordance with the culture of the organization.

For additional information about meetings, please refer to CSAE's publication, *Guide to Better Meetings for Directors of Not-for-Profit Organizations*, at www.csae.com/bookstore.

Minutes

Most corporations keep separate minutes of members' meetings and director meetings, although in the case of smaller organizations, in which the members and directors are the same persons, convenience suggests accepting combined minutes.

Where the board of directors conducts *in camera* meetings, minutes of these meetings should be kept separate; access is restricted unless and until no corporate interest remains in the subject matter.

DUTIES AND RESPONSIBILITIES OF DIRECTORS AND OFFICERS OF NOT-FOR-PROFIT ORGANIZATIONS

Canadian Society of Association Executives

Introduction

For additional information about minutes and minute taking, see the author's article "Do We Have to Put All That in the Minutes?", in the Miller Thomson *Charities and Not-For-Profit* newsletter in May 2011 [www.millerthomson.ca/en/publications/newsletters/charities-and-not-for-profit-newsletter/may-2011]. See also CSAE's *The Minute Takers Handbook*, at www.csae.com/bookstore.

Culture

Just as commercial corporations develop their own culture, so do not-for-profit corporations over time. There is nothing wrong with maintaining that culture, as long as such maintenance does not affect the ability of the corporation, or its directors and officers to meet the requirements of law, its own bylaws, and the challenges outlined in its mission, vision, and objectives.[12]

Profit

Because an entity is a not-for-profit corporation does not necessarily mean that it is not permitted by law to operate at a profit.[13] The main difference that distinguishes a not-for-profit corporation from its commercial counterpart is that if the activities of a not-for-profit corporation produce a profit on its operations, the individual members of the corporation do not personally benefit as is the case of shareholders in a business corporation. Whereas the profit of a commercial corporation accrues to the benefit of the shareholders, the profit from a not-for-profit corporation accrues to the corporation itself.[14][15]

It should be noted that liability for income tax is not automatically excluded simply because the organization is incorporated as a not-for-profit corporation. The *Income Tax Act* contains express provisions as to when tax is or is not payable.[16]

Directors' Liability Exposure

While protection from personal liability flowing from the organization's activities may have been the initial motivation for incorporation, members of the board of directors still face exposure to liability for any of their own actions that are inconsistent with the duties owed by directors to the corporation that such directors serve. Directors must therefore be careful in fulfilling their duties to the corporation (and at times to others) to receive the benefit of such protections as are available. For many of the same reasons that apply to commercial corporations, directors and officers of not-for-profit corporations are subject to most of the same statutory liabilities imposed upon directors and officers of corporations governed by various business corporation statutes of Canada and the provinces.

One of the principal differences between commercial and not-for-profit corporations is that directors of not-for-profit corporations tend to be volunteers from the community in which the not-for-profit corporation serves. That is, persons whose experience in the world of business or commerce is more like that of a consumer or an entrepreneur who is used to making independent decisions unilaterally. As a result, many of these directors are less sophisticated than their commercial counterparts, and mistakenly believe that they are completely shielded from liability merely because they are volunteers or as a result of incorporation.

Therefore, it is important that directors of not-for-profit corporations fully understand their potential personal liability. Furthermore, they must be aware of the duty of care they owe in law—both statutory[17] and common law.[18]

Risk Management

Risk management is all about understanding the hazards that you face and, having considered all of the relevant factors, reacting in accordance with sound judgment. Directors who understand the role, duties, and liabilities of the office as described in this publication, and apply the concepts to govern their own actions accordingly, are unlikely to place themselves in a position where what they do is subject to attack. In the end, successful risk management for a director means that there has been no act upon which an opponent can productively launch an attack.

Role of Directors

As with commercial corporations, a person becomes a director of a not-for-profit corporation in accordance with the corporation's bylaws: by nomination and election by the members of the corporation; by serving in another named office (*ex officio* director[19]); or by appointment. In some jurisdictions, election or appointment of itself is not enough to qualify an individual as a director. The individual must actually consent to hold the office of director.[20]

The statutes providing for incorporation require directors to manage or supervise the management of the affairs of the organization.[21] In addition to this mandate, the directors' powers in a well-organized not-for-profit corporation are generally outlined in the corporation's bylaws. Such bylaws form the cornerstone of the internal governance established by the corporation. Directors initially pass the bylaws, but continuing validity of such governance is contingent upon the members' approval. Directors are bound to act within the limitations set out in the bylaws once they are approved.

Subject to statutory restraints and conditions, the bylaws of a not-for-profit corporation usually cover:

- director qualifications;
- the way a person becomes a director;
- how a director may be removed from office;
- how board of director vacancies are filled;
- how and where meetings of the board of directors may be held;
- quorum for these meetings;
- when directors may and may not exercise their votes; and
- what remuneration, if any, is available to directors.

Role of Directors

Some boards establish policy guidelines for director conduct, both within meetings and relative to the constituents of the corporation. Such guidelines are supplemental to statutory restraints and conditions, and to whatever is set out in the bylaws. Generally, these guidelines address such issues as codes of conduct; form, content, and timing for dealing with conflicts of interest; and procedures, form, content, and timing for dealing with personal conflicts between directors and staff, and between directors. All of these are part of defining the culture of the corporation and the role of its directors.

Regardless of the culture, directors need to be aware that when they attend a meeting of directors or a committee of directors, they are deemed to have consented to any action taken or resolution adopted at the meeting unless they dissent, request the dissent to be entered in the minutes, or gives a written dissent. If not present, directors are deemed to have consented unless they give written dissent to the corporation promptly after becoming aware of the action or resolution.[22]

Duties of Directors

Duty of Knowledge

A director of a corporation, whether not-for-profit or otherwise, must know certain aspects about that corporation.

Although various jurisdictions have different requirements as to content (and identifying labels: articles, charter, letters patent, memorandum, and so on), the constating documents[23] outline the fundamental purpose for the corporation's existence. At a minimum, the director must be constantly aware of the content, though not necessarily the detail, of the constating documents. The director must also be aware of the requirements of the internal governance mechanisms—generally known as the bylaws—by which the corporation operates. Such awareness can only be the result of initial understanding and regular refreshing the recollection of the content of these "cornerstones" of the corporation.

Similarly, directors must understand what the corporation does in practice; that is, how the corporation puts its purposes into action.

In practical terms, orientation of new board members is considered a fundamental prerequisite to full participation in the board processes; regular refreshing and updating of all board members is provided for directors in many organizations (as it should be for all such organizations). Likewise, all board members must consider that the duties of office include an obligation to review, at least annually, these fundamental documents. In every directors' meeting, best practices of boards include at least some education about the corporation operations so that directors can fully understand how mission, vision, and objectives translate into action.

Duties of Directors

Just as there is a need to periodically reflect on the mission, vision, and objectives, directors must also formally review the constating documents and bylaws to ensure that they each remain consistent to the organization's purpose. In particular, the bylaws are the servants of the corporation's work. Although some parts of the bylaws are prescribed by the law of the incorporating jurisdiction, many parts should always support, not inhibit, the fundamental purposes and activity of the corporation. Because of the stable foundation that the bylaws provide to the corporation, alterations should not be undertaken lightly or hastily, but only after careful reflection on the possible and available alternatives.

It must be noted that the bylaws govern the internal workings of the corporation, and until altered in accordance with the appropriate amendment provisions, directors must comply with their terms. This applies not only to the substance of the particulars, but also to the timing as outlined in the bylaws.

Duty of Care

A director of a not-for-profit corporation has a duty in the performance of the activities of the corporation to act in accordance with a minimum standard of care, and may incur personal liability where the conduct falls short of this criterion. In business corporations, this standard test of care is an objective one generally expressed as a standard of care that a reasonably prudent person would exercise under similar circumstances. This objective standard has been codified in the legislation of some provinces that governs business corporations.

Canada,[24] British Columbia,[25] Saskatchewan,[26] Manitoba,[27] Ontario,[28] and Newfoundland[29] have codified an objective standard of care similar to that found in the legislation governing business corporations. For example, the *British Columbia Societies Act* provides:

A Director of a society shall:

a. act honestly and in good faith and in the best interests of the society; and

b. exercise the care, diligence and skill of a reasonably prudent person, in exercising his powers and performing his duties as a director.[30]

The *Canada* and *Ontario NFP Acts* expressly provide that this standard is absolute, and no provision in a contract, constating document, bylaw, or resolution may limit the obligation to comply with the statute and regulations.

Where no objective standard is codified, directors of a not-for-profit corporation in that jurisdiction must discharge their duty by meeting a standard of care that has been defined by the courts. This more subjective standard that must be met is "conduct that may reasonably be expected from a person of such knowledge and experience as the identified director."[31] What emerges from this is that a director with more skill, sophistication, and experience faces a greater standard and a greater risk of personal liability than another director who might lack such specific expertise. As a result, a lawyer, accountant, or other professional must be aware of the higher standard that is expected of someone with such qualifications.

Where the corporation is a charitable organization, an even higher standard of care may be exacted. Directors of charitable organizations are generally held to the same standard of care as a trustee in managing a charitable trust. It is trite law that trustees have a higher duty to the organization than would be the case of a person who does not serve in that capacity.

In British Columbia, a director must conform to the higher standard that a reasonably prudent person must exercise under the same circumstances.[32]

A director who acts honestly and meets these standards of conduct and care will not be liable for simple errors of business judgment that occur while performing the duties of the office. In the case of the *Canada NFP Act*, the *Saskatchewan Act*, and the *Ontario NFP Act*,[33] a director is afforded a reasonable diligence defence as defined in the statute.

Duty of Skill and Prudence

In most jurisdictions, there is no minimum required level of skill or prudence for a director of a not-for-profit corporation. The level of skill required of each director depends on that director's responsibilities within the organization, and the individual skills and experience brought to the position. Where a director has a particular level of expertise, that level must be used in the best

Duties of Directors

interests of the organization. As already noted, no liability is imposed for mere errors in business judgment.

To discharge the duty of prudence, a director must act with practicality and not necessarily expertise in mind. The duty of prudence forces a director to act cautiously and anticipate any probable consequences of any course of action that the organization may choose to undertake.

Duty of Diligence

To discharge the duty of diligence, a director must act in the best interests of the corporation and must be as fully informed as reasonably possible with respect to all aspects of the corporation. As such, directors are accountable to the corporation and must act prudently and reasonably in attempting to preserve the integrity and reputation of the corporation.

In the practical order, the duty of diligence involves becoming thoroughly acquainted with the organization's purpose and policies, what tasks are delegated and to whom, and an awareness of the organization's operations. One of the most significant parts of the duty of diligence requires a director generally to exercise the level of care of an ordinary person, and for this purpose:

- to review the agenda and supporting material in advance of each meeting of the directors and any committee to which appointed;
- to attend meetings of the board and committees to which appointed;
- to be prepared to discuss the business before the meeting in a prepared and knowledgeable way; and
- to vote (unless excluded by reason of conflict of interest or other prohibition) on matters that come before the meeting.

If attending the applicable meeting is not possible, the director should review the minutes of the meeting and other financial statements of the organization in order to stay informed. This is particularly important when an illegal or similar act is undertaken at a meeting. The absent director may be liable unless he or she immediately registers a dissent.

Duty to Manage

The board of directors of a not-for-profit corporation has the duty to manage the affairs of the organization, and to apply the bylaws of the organization. This managerial duty includes, but is not limited to:

- electing officers (where so authorized);
- appointing and supervise staff;
- establishing policies and provide guidance;
- complying with legal requirements;
- acquiring adequate knowledge of the business and functioning of the organization; and
- enacting bylaws as necessary and useful to the operations of the organization.

There is a distinction, and it should be a clearly delineated, between the duties and obligations of the directors and those of the staff. In broad and general terms, directors are responsible for establishing policies, management for implementing them, and directors for measuring management's implementation of those policies.

The actual implementation of the duty to manage the organization can occasionally result in conflict between the directors and senior employees. Such internal conflicts often arise when directors attempt to manage operations, or when senior employees exceed their operational authority as granted by the board of directors. This conflict is the result of misunderstanding of the respective roles of directors and the senior employees.

Fiduciary Duty

A fiduciary within an organization is a person who maintains a position of trust. Where such a position exists, there is a higher standard of care. Directors of business corporations and not-for-profit corporations alike are subject to common-law fiduciary obligations. The imperative of these obligations in the corporate context requires the person to: act honestly and in good faith; be loyal to and to act in the best interest of the corporation; avoid any conflict of interest; and subordinate every personal interest to those of the corporation. This duty, when it exists, applies to all organizations in all jurisdictions.

Duties of Directors

One of the most important features of the fiduciary duty is the obligation to avoid acting in such a way that personal interests conflict with the interests of the corporation and, more specifically, those interests of the corporation that the director must protect. For this reason, a breach of fiduciary duty can occur even in cases in which a director is acting in good faith.[34]

Even where the bylaws of a not-for-profit corporation permit its directors to enter into contracts with the corporation that would otherwise result in a conflict of interest, the fiduciary obligation of the director may prevail over the permission contained in such bylaws.[35]

Duties as Trustees

The courts have not conclusively held that directors of not-for-profit organizations are automatically trustees, but in one case the directors of a charitable foundation were found to be in breach of trust by reason of having made an improper investment for the foundation. Directors of charitable organizations have been held to be subject to the same standard of care to which a trustee would be held. For example, a director of a charitable corporation in Ontario is subject to the *Charities Accounting Act*.[36] Imposing this standard of care to directors of a charitable corporation means that such directors are subject to the higher standard of a reasonable and prudent person in managing that person's own affairs; it is important to note that this is an objective, not a subjective, standard.

One of the reasons that the distinction between trustees and directors is important is that charity trustees are prohibited from being paid, even for work performed in a professional capacity. Underlying this conclusion is the concept that a person may not profit from his or her position as director. Therefore, a trustee can only be paid a fair and reasonable allowance where it is sanctioned by a court.

Investment Powers

Directors of not-for-profit corporations face potential liability with respect to loss on the investment of corporation funds. As a minimum, the board of directors must develop investment policies that include establishing acceptable levels of risk, and then ensuring that those undertaking the investments comply with the policies. Regular and possibly frequent status reports of investments is generally a minimum requirement.

The board of directors must ensure that it has sufficient specialized proficiency to invest corporate funds, otherwise it may be required to enlist the assistance of outside experts. Even where outside expertise is necessary, directors should undertake critical reviews of financial reports at frequent intervals and, correspondingly, must enact bylaws providing for the appropriate investment of corporate funds.

Delegation by Directors

As in the case of commercial corporations, only a restricted type of responsibilities may be wholly delegated by directors of not-for-profit corporations. Delegation alone does not automatically relieve the director from liability regarding delegated tasks. On the contrary, when tasks are delegated, a director continues to be responsible for the resulting actions. For example, although an investment manager is retained to assist generating income or increasing capital value, the ultimate responsibility for managing a charity's assets cannot be delegated.

Delegation is generally best done through adopting policies containing sufficient detail that the delegate has adequate guidance, yet sufficient flexibility that he or she can adapt to the demands of the conditions that apply in practice.[37]

The extent to which a director may delegate responsibilities is subject to statutory limitations,[38] and otherwise is governed by the test of what a prudent person would do under the same circumstances. The director must maintain a supervisory role and cannot blindly rely on the delegated person, committee, officer, or member who actually performs the delegated task.

The services of experts—investment counsellors, trust officers, lawyers, accountants—are often used where directors lack adequate knowledge and experience. Where experts are not members or officers of the organization, directors are under a further duty to ensure that these outside parties have adequate and sufficient qualifications for the task involved.

Duties of Directors

Duty to Avoid Conflicts of Interest

When an individual has a personal interest in the same subject matter as the corporation of which he or she is a director, a conflict of interest arises. As already noted, the fiduciary obligation of a director to the corporation requires the person to act in the best interest of the corporation at all times. A conflict may also arise where a person is a director of two corporations that are involved in the same transaction; the conflict occurs because the director owes a fiduciary duty to both organizations.

It is obvious that a conflict of interest may arise from a wide variety of circumstances, and it is impossible to isolate in this publication how each conflict must be resolved. In most cases, these interests are measurable in direct or indirect pecuniary terms; this section will focus on such incidents. In any event, regard must be had to the relevant statutory provisions.[39]

It should be emphasized that there is nothing inherently wrong with a conflict of interest. Problems arise only when a person who has such a conflict fails to place the personal interest second, behind that of the corporation. It should also be noted that, in the case of a conflict because the person is a director of two corporations involved in the same transactions, the person may not give priority to either corporation, but unless affiliated must remain neutral to both.

It may also be a conflict of interest for directors to receive direct or indirect benefits to their business or property outside of the actual transaction. Directors are also in a conflict of interest where relatives, friends, or co-workers benefit from their actions as a director. Similarly, a director may receive social or political gain, or may benefit from a corporate opportunity of which the director learns in advance of others by reason of the director's position.

The penalty for failure to act appropriately when a conflict of interest exists can range from a quasi-criminal conviction[40] to a common-law requirement to deliver to the corporation any benefit gained from the transaction. Resolving a conflict issue is based on the proposition that a person may not profit from the position of director at the expense of the organization. For example, when contracting with the organization, a director may not use the position to negotiate terms that are personally advantageous but are not of at least equal advantage to the corporation. An independent third party is not so limited, and would not be barred from negotiating a personal advantage at the expense of the corporation.

A director's gain through a conflict of interest situation will not automatically lead to liability. Statutory provisions generally provide that liability for conflicts of interest may be avoided where a director declares personal interest in a particular transaction or event at the directors' meeting at which the matter first arises or, where the director is not present at that meeting, at the next meeting that the director attends.[41] Similarly, when a director makes the statutory disclosure and does not participate in or influence the decision-making process, the director may retain any profit from the transaction.[42]

Bylaws of many not-for-profit corporations will provide mechanisms for ratifying contracts where directors have a personal involvement, and will outline the circumstances under which such might be granted.

Duty to Act Within Scope of Authority

Directors must know both the scope of their own authority and the permitted activities of a corporation. In a not-for-profit corporation as in a commercial corporation, a combination of the objects, bylaws, and resolutions of the board of directors outlines the permitted activities of the corporation and the scope of authority of an individual director. Personal liability can attach to any director whenever that director, by positive action or by neglect, permits the corporation to carry on activities that are *ultra vires* of the corporation (beyond the power or authority of the corporation).[43] An individual may also incur personal liability when acting outside the scope of the actual authority that has been granted to him or her as noted in the corporation's records.

Avoiding personal liability in such situations is simple and straightforward. In the case of *ultra vires* activity, the director must oppose the action during the directors' meeting at which the action was authorized (if not present, at the first meeting attended thereafter), and should demand that that opposition be recorded in that meeting's minutes.

Liabilities of Directors

Criminal Liability

The Canada *Criminal Code*, as well as other federal and provincial statutes, defines criminal and quasi-criminal action of directors. While these statutes are rarely invoked, there can be very serious consequences if a director is found liable under any of them. Consequences include fines, imprisonment, or both. The most common examples from a director's perspective are conspiracy and fraud, as a director may be liable where the organization commits fraud where it was authorized, permitted, or allowed by the director.

The *Criminal Code* was amended in a way that extends the existing rules for attributing acts of directors to the corporations, thereby making corporations liable for certain of the acts of directors.[44] This amendment also imposes a legal duty on all persons directing work—and this likely includes directors—to take reasonable steps to ensure the safety of works and the public.[45] The *Criminal Code* was also amended to create the criminal offence of threats or retaliation against whistle-blowing employees who disclose unlawful conduct of a corporate employer or its directors.[46]

Civil Liability

The commission of a civil offence may also lead to the personal liability of a director, but generally only where the director has personally participated in the offence. Again, generally there will be no civil liability where there has been no involvement on the part of the director. By contrast, a director may be personally liable upon expressly authorizing the wrongful act that is the subject of the civil offence.

Directors should ensure that any contract entered into by the organization is carefully worded so that it is clear that it is the organization *and not any individual director* that is entering into the contract or transaction. Directors act as

Liabilities of Directors

agents for the organization but do not themselves directly contract with other parties. In order to avoid ambiguity in such cases, the words "by," "pro," or "per" should precede the director's signature in any relevant documents.

Statutory Liabilities

While a detailed review of every potential area of liability is beyond the scope of this publication, directors should be aware of the liability that exists locally under the incorporating statutes of their jurisdictions.[47]

Hundreds of federal and provincial statutes in Canada impose some statutory liability on officers and directors of corporations, both commercial and not-for-profit. These potential areas of liability arise in a wide variety of circumstances. For example, the *Canada Corporations Act* contains penalties for directors of federally incorporated organizations that fail to comply with the provisions of the *Act* and, on conviction, can be fined up to $1,000 and/or imprisoned up to one year.[48]

Provincial legislation contains similar provisions for breaches of respective relevant provincial statutes.[49]

In Ontario, for example, a director may be liable:

- where the location of the head office has changed;[50]
- where there has been a failure to file a notice of special resolution that the number of directors has changed;[51]
- where there is a failure to keep records of proceedings and documents at the head office or other authorized location of the corporation so that they are open for inspection by the directors;[52] or
- if a director refuses to permit a person entitled thereto to inspect the minutes, documents or registers of the corporation during normal business hours.[53]

The *Canada Corporations Act* also imposes liability on directors of its corporations. For example, a director faces a fine of $100 per day where the director knowingly and wilfully permits a corporation to default on its obligation to file annual returns.[54] Directors may also be liable if they knowingly authorize the issue of the corporate seal, or the company name is not legible on notices, advertisements, bills of exchange, promissory notes, invoices, or other similar documents. Similar kinds of provisions are contained in the *Canada NFP Act* and the *Ontario NFP Act*.

Employee and Workplace Liability

Various statutes outline the duties of employers and directors of employers to employees in the workplace, including not-for-profit corporation employers. Directors are required, at the very least, to exercise due diligence to ensure that the corporation is not violating any of these statutes. Some statutes subject directors to penalty sanctions where the director caused or acquiesced to the breach of the organization's statutory duty to the employee. Directors may also be held personally liable for certain wages and benefits owed to employees in some cases.

Directors can be jointly and severally liable for up to six months of unpaid wages and vacation pay (12 months in the case of the *Ontario Corporations Act*[55]) if a corporation is bankrupt or insolvent or where the debt is owed and has not been satisfied. This duty continues for Ontario directors for six months after the person ceases to be a director. In Saskatchewan, directors are liable for all debts payable to each employee for services to the corporation while they are directors.[56]

A number of other federal[57] and provincial[58] statutes govern the liability of directors with respect to their employees and the workplace environment.

Income Tax Liability

A number of statutes create obligations on employers to collect and remit taxes to the government. Directors may be liable to pay any amount of employee taxes that are not remitted, including penalties and interest.[59] The *Income Tax Act* imposes penalties on a director who allows an offence to occur by a not-for-profit corporation, including a registered charity failing to maintain records to verify deductible amounts. This offence could result in a fine of up to $10,000 or imprisonment for six months. Directors of not-for-profit corporations must ensure that all legislative guidelines are complied with so that the corporation may enjoy all the tax benefits to which it is entitled. Personal liability may result where the director's action or inaction leads to the loss of certain charitable tax benefits.

Liabilities of Directors

There are numerous other heads of liability under the *Income Tax Act*. However, directors are entitled to a due-diligence defence if they can show that they have exercised a reasonable degree of skill and care as would be exercised in similar circumstances by a reasonably prudent person. This due diligence, which can lead to a complete defence to personal liability, could take the form of something as simple as requiring the executive director or another employee to report to the board, on a periodic basis, perhaps monthly or quarterly, confirming that all required remittances have been sent to the appropriate governmental authority.

Other federal tax-related statutes impose liability on directors of not-for-profit corporations, including the *Excise Tax Act* (which imposes liability on directors for failing to collect and remit the Goods and Services Tax), *Employment Insurance Act* (where directors can be jointly and severally liable for failure to deduct and remit premiums), and *Canada Pension Plan Act* (for failure to collect Canada Pension Plan contributions).[60] Further, numerous provincial statutes impose some type of tax liability on directors of not-for-profit corporations.[61]

A director can only escape personal liability for such liability incurred during the director's term, after two years of leaving his or her position as director, but no director will be held liable for the failure of previous directors to remit payroll or other taxes.

A 1997 case has held that the test of due diligence is not uniform for all directors in a not-for-profit corporation, and therefore courts may take into account the circumstances under which a director serves.[62]

In another case, a not-for-profit corporation failed to remit payroll deductions for almost two years. The Tax Court decided that the level of due diligence required of directors of not-for-profit corporations under the *Income Tax Act* is lower than that of other corporations.[63] This case might well be limited in a future prosecution to its own facts; the prudent course for directors is to ensure remittances of deductions are faithfully made by the corporation.

Environmental Liability

Environmental responsibility is becoming increasingly important for directors of all corporations. Both the common law and legislation have increased the potential liability of directors of all corporations where environmental problems may be encountered. Although for many organizations environmental liability is entirely hypothetical without any practical exposure, such issues are very real, very important, and potentially very costly for not-for-profit corporations that are hunting, fishing, or snowmobile clubs.

For example, a director of a corporation has been found liable for failure to comply with a statutory duty under the *Ontario Water Resources Act*.[64] Only those directors who could demonstrate that they had exercised due diligence were found not liable. A number of federal statutes set out offences that impose specific liability on directors and this liability can be very stringent in some circumstances; therefore, it is important that all corporations establish safeguards and controls.[65]

A number of provincial statutes impose liability on directors. For example, the *Ontario Environmental Protection Act* extends liability to a director even where a corporation has not been prosecuted or convicted.[66] A director will be liable where the corporation engages in an activity that results in the discharge of a contaminant into a natural environment. A due-diligence defence is available. Factors to be considered include whether:

- directors have established a pollution prevention system;
- there was supervision or inspection;
- there were improvements in business methods;
- the directors ensured that corporate officers were instructed to set up sufficient systems within industry terms and practices;
- officers were to report back periodically; and
- officers were instructed to report any substantial non-compliance to the directors.[67]

Liabilities of Directors

Business Practices

Directors of not-for-profit corporations will face liability where any actions are taken that have the effect of misleading purchasers. Directors will be prosecuted if they participate in the commission of an offence or allow the offence to occur under the *Competition Act* or the *Business Practices Act*. Where a not-for-profit corporation is involved in the sale of goods and services, directors may be liable for misleading advertising, double ticketing, promotional contests, production/delivery of spam, or e-commerce and other trade practices.

Protection of Directors

In addition to adherence by directors to the appropriate standards of care, a number of protective measures are available, individually and collectively designed to minimize the exposure of directors of not-for-profit corporations to legal liability. Directors should be aware that for the most part, these protections are voluntary at the instance of the corporation, and a later board of directors may not continue the protection. A cautious director may insist that the corporation, by formal contract, undertake to provide and continue protection indefinitely, both by way of indemnity and funded by the provision of insurance coverage.

Indemnification

Indemnification means that the corporation will compensate the director for any loss incurred for the liabilities arising from the performance of the director's duties, within the scope of that director's authority, except those arising from wilfully negligent actions. The incorporating statutes of not-for-profit corporations generally permit or provide for the indemnification of directors. A director can be indemnified for all charges, costs, and expenses sustained or incurred as a result of any claim or other proceeding against the director.[68] It is even possible for a director to receive an indemnity where there has been negligence, as long as the director has acted in good faith.

British Columbia[69] provides for a broad indemnity for directors of not-for-profit organizations so it is unnecessary for members of the organization to ratify the indemnity clause as is required under the *Canada Corporations Act*. Similarly, the *Canada NFP Act*[70] and the *Ontario NFP Act*[71] have removed the necessity of obtaining member approval for indemnities. These latter statutes also

Protection of Directors

permit the corporation to advance monies to a protected director or officer while the matter proceeds.[72]

There are complications in providing indemnification for directors of charitable organizations. Until quite recently, the Public Guardian and Trustee in Ontario took the position that, because directors of charitable organizations are trustees and cannot profit from that position, they cannot be remunerated for their services; that indemnity insurance must be considered as a form of remuneration; and that a charity in Ontario had to seek court approval before providing an indemnity clause to its directors.[73] Regrettably, the courts adopted this view of the Public Trustee.[74]

Early in 2001, the Lieutenant-Governor-in-Council enacted Ontario Regulation 4/01 to provide that acts authorized by this Regulation, that would otherwise have required Court approval, should be treated for all purposes as though they had such Court approval. Among the acts authorized were indemnities to directors and corresponding indemnity insurance. These benefits are not without limitation.[75] Specifically, there are five factors that directors must consider before giving an indemnity or purchasing insurance:

1. The degree of risk to which the director or corporation is or may be exposed.
2. Whether, in practice, the risk cannot be eliminated or significantly reduced by means other than the indemnity or insurance.
3. Whether the amount or cost of the insurance is reasonable in relation to the risk.
4. Whether the cost of the insurance is reasonable in relation to the revenue available to the corporation.
5. Whether it advances the administration and management of the property to give the indemnity or purchase the insurance.

It should be noted that these factors are instructive guidance to directors in considering *any* decision having financial implications.

The purpose of indemnification is to encourage skilled directors to participate in not-for-profit organizations.

It is important to note that an indemnity is only effective if the corporation is in a financial position to honour it when the director needs the protection. If the corporation does not have adequate funds to indemnify when it is needed, either in its own treasury or by way of insurance moneys, then the indemnification is illusory.

Insurance

Not only is an indemnity only as good as the financial stability of the organization, but indemnification also does not eliminate the risk of all liabilities, including breaches of standard of care, breaches of certain statutes, and situations where the corporation itself is suing the director. Notwithstanding these limitations, directors' liability insurance can often provide sufficient protection for these situations.

The expenses involved with directors' liability insurance vary with the type of activity in which the organization participates. With the increasing sophistication of directors in these organizations, there is increasing pressure for added protection through insurance programs.

Directors' liability insurance can be maintained in one of two ways: either through the corporation, where the premiums are paid by the corporation; or by the director personally, where the premiums are paid by either the director or the corporation. The decision as to which of the two types is used, or even both, is a policy decision to be made by the individual corporation itself.

The *Canada Corporations Act* is silent with respect to directors' liability insurance. However, the *Canada NFP Act*,[76] the *BC Society Act*,[77] and the *Ontario NFP Act*[78] expressly allow for the purchase of insurance by not-for-profit organizations to protect directors from personal liability.

While it is becoming common for all organizations to have this form of protection,[79] the cost of such insurance is increasingly prohibitive for many. Furthermore, not all types of liability are covered, including acts that are *ultra vires* and where conflict of interest situations have resulted in personal profits for the directors.

Protection of Directors

Independent Advice

Directors must act within the scope of their authority and in the best interests of the corporation. Sometimes this calls for directors to seek independent advice, particularly where knowledge is needed in a field where directors do not have any expertise. One such example is in the investment of corporate funds. Where independent advice is sought, directors should ensure that properly qualified individuals are asked for their expertise.

Disclosure of Competing Interests

Perhaps the easiest way to avoid personal liability is for a director to disclose to the board, at the earliest opportunity, all situations in which a conflict of interest may arise. This is particularly true for any personal interests related to the transactions of the organization. Disclosure should take place regardless of whether the interests are direct or indirect.

Legislation in Canada and several provinces set out the provisions for disclosure in conflict of interest situations, and the interest should be disclosed at the first opportunity and declared at the meeting of the board of directors. Further, the director is precluded from voting on any contract, transaction, or matter in which the director has any interest, no matter how remote.[80] And as already noted, these requirements also apply where the person is a director of two (or more) organizations unless they are affiliated.

Impact of Ratification

Directors can be protected from personal liability where members of the organization ratify their actions. For example, where a director fully discloses a personal interest in a contract, the members may ratify the contract and move liability to the corporation or its creditors from the personal liability of the director. The membership exerts a measure of control over the management of the organization by the directors and, as such, this ratification provides protection from liability. But it should be noted that it is not possible to protect against *all* claims of third parties.

Due Diligence

Reducing the risk of liability before problems actually occur is probably the most effective form of protection. This *ex ante* form of protection comes in the form of due diligence. Not only can due diligence prevent problems from occurring, it can also prevent a director from accepting a position at an organization where problems have already occurred and currently exist.

There is no exact formula for what proper due diligence should be. Different situations and different organizations will call for different levels of due diligence. However, it is always important for a director to understand the organization, and to know the objects and purposes of the organization. This involves checking the constating documents, the annual reports, the financial statements, and the statutes applicable to the organization.

Furthermore, after accepting a directorship with an organization, the director must still exercise due diligence when carrying out the functions of the organization. Directors must know what the organization is doing, what transactions are occurring, and with what activities the organization is involved. The director must also attend meetings, review materials, discuss the issues with other members of the board and make decisions, as well as ensuring compliance with applicable legislation.

An Effective Board of Directors

An effective board of directors strives to fulfil the purpose of the organization. An effective board will lead to a successful organization, minimize potential liability for the organization, and also limit the liability of directors personally. An organization should develop and keep a report card on its directors. This report card is an assessment of the performance of the board as a whole, and the individual directors. It should serve as a reminder of the purposes and objects of the organization, and should outline the duties and responsibilities of the board and its individual directors. This periodic[81] review should include the steps needed and taken to discharge the duty of due diligence and to act within the appropriate standard of care.

Checklist

A sample checklist, by no means exhaustive and in no particular order, might include the following:

- know the corporate mandate; its mission, vision and objectives; its operations; and its bylaws;
- always act objectively, and in the best interest of the corporation;
- prepare for all board meetings, and all committee meetings of which the director is a member, by reviewing all agenda material including reports;
- attend, and participate in, all board meetings, and all committee meetings of which the director is a member;
- keep careful notes at meetings, and review the minutes of all meetings;
- insist upon the establishment and regular review of operating policies, and monitor staff adherence to them;

An Effective Board of Directors

- obtain outside expert advice whenever necessary;
- disclose all personal dealings as early as practical;
- refrain from voting only where necessary;
- ensure that minutes record directors' disclosures, dissents, or refraining from voting;
- ensure that there are effective internal systems in all areas of corporate activity, particularly accounting;
- consider, in *any* decision having financial implications, the five factors enumerated on page 34.
- avoid possible conflict situations; and
- maintain proper record-keeping system.

Checklist Caution

A final caution regarding this or any other similar checklist: it is neither exhaustive nor a complete shield from liability or criticism. In addition to applying common sense, an effective director understands that there will be times when it is prudent to seek legal or other professional guidance, independent of the organization itself, as to the appropriate course in particular situations.

Endnotes

1. For a high-level summary of a number of the corporate scandals, see http://www.forbes.com/2002/07/25/accountingtracker.html (accessed 29 August 2011).
2. Statutes of Canada 2009, c. 23; proclamation is anticipated by the end of 2011.
3. Statutes of Ontario 2010, c. 15; proclamation is anticipated by the end of 2012.
4. Revised Statutes of Canada, 1970, c. C-32, as amended ("*Canada Corporations Act*").
5. Revise Statutes of Ontario 1990, c.C.38, as amended ("Ontario *Corporations Act*")
6. Also known as "corporations without share capital," or "non share capital corporations." The term "not-for-profit corporation" (which appears to have its origins in the laws of some of the United States) signifies principally that such a corporation has *not* been incorporated *for the purpose* of making a profit, although profit on operations is permissible but is required to be used to advance the objects of the corporation.

    This publication does not attempt to consider issues of the calculation of "profit" for the purposes of income tax, nor does it consider commercial corporations that are operated (intentionally or otherwise) at a financially break-even basis. Whatever other differences there may be, in this publication the term "not-for-profit" is used throughout.
7. These include, but are not limited to, providing a structure for day-to-day business, facilitating fundraising, establishing credibility within its community, and perhaps most importantly to put limits on the liability of persons connected with the organization.
8. Such business counterparts are generally referred to in this publication as "commercial corporations."
9. The Canada NFP Act does not permit *ex officio* directors.
10. The Canada NFP Act, s.128(8), Ontario NFP Act, s.24(7).
11. As "shorthand" in this publication, the term "auditor" includes, as the case requires, the auditor, the "public accountant" (the term used in the Canada NFP Act), and the "person appointed to conduct a review engagement" (an alternative provided in the Ontario NFP Act).
12. For an interesting analysis of differing "cultures" (although, as indicated by its title, it addresses other issues), see an article by Prof. Vic Murray, "Improving Board Performance," published in *The Philanthropist*, Vol.13, No.4.
13. "Profit" for the purposes of this publication may be considered as an excess of receipts over disbursements, although this may not be accurate in the taxation or accounting sense.
14. The Articles, Letters Patent, or other constating documents will almost always require that such profits be devoted to the promotion of the objects of the corporation.
15. One of the exceptions occurs where the remaining property of a social club may be distributed among the members at the time such corporation is wound up.
16. The Income Tax Act of Canada, Revise Statutes of Canada 1985, c.1, as amended; see particularly s.149(1)(l).

17. It is not feasible in this publication to review every federal and provincial statute that imposes some statutory duty or liability on a not-for-profit corporation director, although there are some references to assist understanding of context.
18. This is so-called "judge-made" law, resulting from consistency in decisions of the courts over time, evolving with the times, and representing what is a currently accepted community standard.
19. *Ex-officio* directors share all of the burdens and benefits of all other directors. Contrary to a popular misconception, *ex-officio* directors as a matter of law *always* have the same voting rights as other directors.

    As previously noted, the Canada NFP Act does not permit *ex officio* directors.
20. The Canada NFP Act, s. 128(9), by being present when elected/appointed and not demurring; by written consent; or by acting as a director; see also the Ontario NFP Act, s. 24(8).
21. With specific exceptions, directors have authority to delegate their powers to a managing director or a committee (such as an Executive Committee): Canada NFP Act, s.138; Ontario NFP Act, s.36.
22. The Canada NFP Act, s. 147; Ontario NFP Act, s.45; but note that a dissent is not available to a director who votes in favour of the action or resolution.
23. Constating documents: fundamental documents that are the legal foundation or framework for a corporation. Depending upon the jurisdiction, the initial constating documents have formal titles of "Articles of Association," Articles of Incorporation,""Letters Patent (and Supplementary Letters Patent)'" or "Memorandum of Association." The term includes the bylaws as enacted from time to time.
24. The Canada NFP Act. s.148.
25. *Societies Act*, R.S.B.C. 1996, c. 433.
26. *Non-Profit Corporations Act*, 1995, S.S. 1995, c.N-4.2 ("Saskatchewan Act"),.109.
27. *Corporations Act*, R.S.M. 1987, c.C225, 117(1).
28. The Ontario NFP Act, s.43.
29. *Corporations Act*, R.S.N. 1990, c.C-36, 203(1) (1).
30. *Op.Cit.*, s.25(1).
31. Re *City Equitable Fire Insurance Co.* [1924] All E.R. Rep.485.
32. *Op.Cit.*, s.25(1)(b).
33. The Canada NFP Act, s.149; the Saskatchewan Act, s.109 and s.112.1; and the Ontario NFP Act, s. 44.
34. In one court case, *Native People of Thunder Bay Development Corp. v. Pierre* (1989), 4 D.L.R. 419 (Ont.Div.Ct.), a director of a non-profit housing corporation was found to have breached her fiduciary duty to the corporation where, as a tenant of the corporation, she refused to pay rent to protest a procedural breach by the corporation.
35. *Wedge v. McNeill* (1982) 126 D.L.R. (3rd) 596 (P.E.I.S.C.): reversed on other grounds 142 D.L.R. (3rd) 133 (P.E.I.C.A.).
36. R.S.O. 1990, c.C.10.
37. The Canadian Society of Association Executives has a number of such policies that readers might find instructive.
38. See, for example, the Canada NFP Act, s.138; the Saskatchewan Act, s.102; or the Ontario NFP Act, s.36.
39. See, for example, the *Canada Corporations Act*, s.98; the Canada NFP Act, s.141; Saskatchewan Act, s.107; Ontario *Corporations Act*, s.71; the Ontario NFP Act, s.41.

40. See, for example; the Ontario *Corporations Act*, s. 71(6), where, on conviction a person is liable to a fine of not more than $200; or the Canada NFP Act, s.262, or the Ontario NFP Act, where on conviction, a person is liable to a fine of $5,000 and/or 6 months imprisonment;
41. *Ibid*, s.71(1), (2) which provide:
    (1) Every director of a company who is in any way directly or indirectly interested in a proposed contract or a contract with the company shall declare his or her interest at a meeting of the directors of the company.
    (2) In the case of a proposed contract, the declaration required by this section shall be made at the meeting of the directors at which the question of entering into the contract is first taken into consideration or, if the director is not at the date of that meeting interested in the proposed contract, at the next meeting of the directors held after he or she becomes so interested, and, in a case where the director becomes interested in a contract after it is made, the declaration shall be made at the first meeting of the directors held after he or she becomes so interested.
42. Additional protection is provided in s.71(5) of the Ontario Act: Despite anything in this section, a director is not accountable to the company or to any of its [members] or creditors for any profit realized from such contract and the contract is not by reason only of the director's interest therein voidable if it is confirmed by a majority of the votes cast at a general meeting of the [members] duly called for that purpose and if the director's interest in the contract is declared in the notice calling the meeting. A similar provision is found in s.98 of the Canada *Corporations Act*.
43. Under s.16 of the Canada NFP Act, s.15 of the Saskatchewan Act, and s.15 of the Ontario NFP Act, the concept of *ultra vires* has been eliminated, as corporations have all of the powers of a natural person.
44. Statutes of Canada 2003, Ch. 21, adding sections 22.1 and 22.2, and relevant new definitions, to the *Criminal Code* proclaimed in force effective 31 March 2004.
45. *Ibid*., adding section 217.1, and a number of related new sections and subsections.
46. Statutes of Canada 2004, c. 3, s. 6, adding section 425.1.
47. For a modest expansion on this topic by the author, see "You Mean I Could Be Responsible for That?" published by the Canadian Society of Association Executives in *Association*™ Magazine, Vol. 21, No. 8, February-March 2003, at page 12.
48. Canada *Corporations Act*, s.43; see also references in footnote 42.
49. See for example, Ontario *Corporations Act*, s.331.
50. *Ibid*., s.277.
51. *Ibid*., s.285.
52. *Ibid*., s.304.
53. *Ibid*., s.305.
54. Section 133.
55. *Op.Cit.*, s.81; see also the Canada NFP Act, s.146; the Ontario NFP Act, s.40.
56. Saskatchewan Act, s.106.
57. See, for example, Canada *Pension Plan Act*, *Health Insurance Act*, *Employment Insurance Act*, Canada *Labour Code*.
58. For example, in Ontario, the following Acts would apply: *Employment Standards Act*, *Labour Relations Act*, *Employers and Employee Act*, *Occupational Health and Safety Act*, *Pensions Benefit Act*, *Pay Equity Act*, *Employment Equity Act*, *Ontario Corporations Act*, and *Ontario Cooperative Corporations Act*.
59. *Income Tax Act* Section 227.1.

60. Section 21.1.
61. In Ontario, these would include the Ontario *Retail Sales Tax Act*, Ontario *Corporations Tax Act*, *Goods and Services Tax Act*, and the *Employer Health Tax Act*.
62. *Soper v. The Queen* (1997), F.C.J. No. 881.
63. See *G. Wheeliker et al v. the Queen*.
64. *R. v. Bata Industries Ltd.* (1992), 9 O.R. (3rd) 29; varied (1993) 14 O.R. (3rd) 354 (Gen.Div.).
65. See, for example, the Canadian *Environmental Protection Act*, the *Fisheries Act*, the *Transportation and Dangerous Goods Act*, and the *Hazardous Products Act*.
66. Other provincial legislation in Ontario for example includes the Ontario *Water Resources Act*, the *Pesticides Act*, and the *Gasoline Act*.
67. *R. v. Bata Industries*, supra.
68. See, for example, the Canada *Corporations Act*, s.93; the Canada NFP Act, s.151; Ontario *Corporations Act*, s.80, the Ontario NFP Act, s.46.
69. *Society Act*, Op.Cit., s.30.
70. Section 151.
71. Section 46.
72. Subsections 151(2) and 46(2), respectively.
73. This position of the Ontario Public Guardian and Trustee is difficult to understand. In most cases, directors of not-for-profit corporations including charitable corporations devote significant time and effort to serving the corporation without reward of any kind. It seems unconscionable that directors should be exposed to risk simply because they volunteer to serve their communities in this way, and would not be exposed to personal liability except that they so serve.
74. See *Re: David Feldman Charitable Trust*, endnote 21; see also *Re: Toronto Humane Society and Ontario (Public Trustee)* (1987), 40 D.L.R. (4th) 111 (High Court).
75. In addition to the five specific factors noted in the text, Ontario Regulation 4/01 requires that:
    - a director cannot be indemnified for failure to act honestly and in good faith in the performance of the director's duties;
    - neither the indemnity nor the insurance may impair any person's right to bring action against the director;
    - the purchase of insurance cannot unduly impair the carrying out of the purposes of the corporation;
    - the indemnity may not be paid, and the insurance not purchased, if doing so would render the corporation insolvent.
76. Subsection 151(6).
77. Subsection 30(5).
78. Subsection 46(6).
79. In its 1996 "Association Benchmarks & Policies Report," a survey conducted by Canadian Society of Association Executives as to how its members do their work, 80 percent of the 414 respondents carried insurance at an average annual cost of about $2,470.
80. The B.C. *Society Act*, s. 7 calls for the disclosure of any conflict "fully and promptly" to the Society. The Canada NFP Act and the Ontario NFP Act require disclosure at meeting when matter first considered or thereafter, at first meeting at which director is present or when director becomes interested.
81. Annual or biennial reviews are recommended.

About the Author

Hugh Kelly has over forty-five years of experience as a lawyer for clients on education, health law, and charitable and not-for-profit organizations matters. His extensive work with not-for-profit organizations has included charitable and volunteer groups, private clubs (athletic and social), and other incorporated and unincorporated groups.

He addresses not-for-profit organizations' responsibilities as governed by the Corporations Acts, and the Not-for-Profit Corporations Acts at both federal and provincial levels. He also advises on governance and organizational concerns, as well as general not-for-profit issues for such organizations.

CSAE wishes to thank the following corporations for their support

Morneau Shepell

MULTIVIEW